Study Guide
for
TOPICS AND SKILLS
IN ENGLISH

GW00802115

Study Guide
for
TOPICS AND SKILLS
IN ENGLISH

Vivien Barr and Clare Fletcher

HODDER AND STOUGHTON
LONDON SYDNEY AUCKLAND TORONTO

British Library Cataloguing in Publication Data

Barr, Vivien
  Topics and skills in English.
  1. English language—Text-books for foreigners
  I. Title   II. Fletcher, Clare
  428.2′4   PE1128

ISBN 0 340 28709 8

Typeset in 10/11pt Century Schoolbook (Monophoto) by Macmillan India Ltd.

Printed in Hong Kong for Hodder and Stoughton Educational, a division of Hodder and Stoughton Ltd, Mill Road, Dunton Green, Sevenoaks, Kent, by Colorcraft Ltd.

Contents

Encourage students to indicate the employer's business if this is not immediately obvious from the name of the company. If students have not worked, they should put *none* by previous employment (also useful for *military record, criminal convictions, books published*, etc. Look at real forms for other headings.).

Section 4: References

Look at the reference for Mr John Campbell in Unit 6 *Writing Formal Letters* on p. 58. Point out that it is often a good idea to give the referee some information about the job so that he can write an appropriate reference.

Vocabulary an alternative to *position* for a referee is *status*.

Section 5: Making the form fit you

Encourage students to make appropriate changes and to give a little more information than is asked for, if appropriate (as with explaining the employer's business).

Point out that the advantage of the *Personal Record* is that all the sections and headings are relevant to them.

Section 6: Covering letter

Students can also include in the covering letter reasons why they want the job. If there are 'acceptable' reasons it is worth including them and any expression of enthusiasm about the job; however if students find it a struggle to put anything like this, it is better left out.

Section 7: Personal record

Students should fill this out in pencil first, concentrating on use of space and neatness. The final copy should have no errors!

Introduce the final section on *Personal Record* by discussing which headings on the application form are not suitable for their Personal Records. This may vary from student to student.

Contrast *personal* and *personnel*: meaning, spelling and pronunciation.

Focus students' attention on the importance of good layout.

Deal with how to describe interests and the kind of abilities and interests which are relevant, eg *driving licence, languages, voluntary work, positions of responsibility on committees, membership of societies, part-time classes.*

This aspect is not covered in the work on forms and needs to be dealt with here. Encourage students to use the word 'interests' rather than hobbies. Anticipate work on interviews by practising 'talking about yourself.'

Unit 9 Interviews

The unit follows the process of being invited for a job interview, replying, preparing beforehand, and actually being interviewed. Students who are likely to be interviewed for a course rather than a job can refer back to the letter in Unit 6 *Writing formal letters* page 65 inviting someone to an interview at a college. Sections 2 and 3 are directly relevant to course- as well as job-interviews. Much of the rest also applies, with changes of detail.

Section 1: Getting an interview

This begins the case-study of the laboratory assistant vacancy at Deacon & Co. Ltd. The section introduces the idea of shortlisting and the role of the Personnel Officer. Another point to notice is that the letter asks for confirmation. This, of course, can be given either by phone or in writing. Ask students what would be different in the letter if it was written to one of the other candidates (name, address, time). Use the map to practise directions.

Section 2: Replying to the letter

The case study continues. Make sure students understand that they are now in the position of the Personnel Officer, waiting to hear from the candidates. The three letters provide models of what to write when confirming, declining or asking for another time and day. With the third letter, discuss what constitutes an acceptable reason for asking for another day or time. Point out the risks involved. Students could make brief notes on the structure of the letter. For example, it mentions

> letter received
> interview, date and time
> job
> explains the problem fully
> suggests other days and times
> asks for a different time
> apologises

Students are asked to fill in the responses on the Personnel Officer's chart. They would not normally be expected to take this role but this checks that they have understood the answer in each case and shows them the important steps in the process of receiving applications, shortlisting, asking candidates to come for interview and recording replies.

In order to prepare students for exercises B and C, you could ask them to make brief notes on all the letters and both phone calls. The first call is more complicated, and notes often remind students of the information they have to give.

A Key

> Somer – not coming
> Kent – asked for another day and time
> Grant – asked for another time
> Bristol – confirmed
> Arnold – confirmed

Section 3: Planning the journey

This shows the importance of practical details: planning the journey and allowing plenty of time to find your way in an unfamiliar area or building. The timetable can be exploited in several ways:

practise talking in 24-hour clock times
passenger and booking clerk pairwork – asking for and giving timetable
 information
talking about how long a journey takes
using time prepositions: I need to be there *by* . . .
                        I need to be there *within* . . .

As well as planning the journey, candidates need to take with them necessary details, such as company name and address, the name of the person to ask for, directions inside the building and any certificates they might have (point out that these should only be produced if they are asked for). Candidates also need to prepare suitable questions to ask at the interview (Section 5 gives some help with this).

Key

> *Notes for John Bristol*
> Job: Laboratory asst.
> Interview day: Tuesday   Date: 22nd January   Time: 1020
> Firm + address: Deacon & Co. Ltd.
>   40–44 Turners Lane, Willington, Harts.
> (suggest including tel. no. It is best if candidates take the letter from the
>   firm with them)
> Leave home at: 0910 approx
> Train leaves from Giggiston at 0929
>   arrives at Willington at 0948

Discuss whether or not it is advisable to get the earlier train, 0909 from Giggiston, in case there is a cancellation.

The teacher can extend this exercise on planning the journey and taking details about the firm. Use a local train timetable. Take the part of an employment agency, ringing up to give details of an interview. Students have to take down the details and use the timetable to work out when to leave home. These are the kind of details students can be asked to write down:

Job:
Firm's name and address:
Name of the employment agency:
Day and time of interview:
Who to ask for:
Directions inside the building:
Nearest station:
Approximate distance from the station:

You can extend the exercise still further by organising pairwork, with the person from the Agency having the details on a card.

Section 4: Preparing for an interview

This encourages the student to assess him/herself realistically and to anticipate what an employer will be looking for in an interview for a particular job.

C
The listening exercise gives a model for how to sound willing, how to use what you have learned in contexts other than work if you have had no experience.

E What kind of questions are you likely to be asked?
This leads into the next section and encourages students to think about the kinds of questions they may be asked.

Key

Suggested questions:
a) Are you punctual?
b) Are you often absent from work?
c) How long have you been in England?
d) Why do you want this job?
   Why does this type of work appeal to you?
e) Have you got any questions you would like to ask?
   Are there any questions you would like to ask?
   Is there anything you would like to know?

Section 5: Pattern of an interview

This section suggests that interviews follow a pattern. Of course it is impossible to predict exactly but it is helpful if students can anticipate what is behind the questions, and if they realise that the interviewer is unlikely to ask a real question at the beginning.

If possible, arrange for students to be interviewed individually by someone they have never seen before. The feedback from both sides will be useful. Encourage students to bring in a cassette of their own to record the interview and then the teacher can listen to it and give advice, which can also be recorded. If you can arrange it, record each interview on video tape.

Section 6: Further practice

A Key

1 (d)	2 (a)	3 (f)	4 (e)
5 (c)	6 (b)		

B Key

How big is the company?
What would be my working hours?
How many days' holiday would I get?
What is the basic pay?
(if applicable) Is there any overtime?

Unit 10 Alphabetical order

Work should be done regularly – little and often – with other types of activity in between. A one-hour session is probably long enough (for some students a shorter time may be better). You could work on this unit at the same time as Unit 2 *Using the Telephone*. A two-hour session might contain one hour on each.

Section 1: *Check your skill* shows each individual which parts of the Unit s/he needs.

The main emphasis of the unit is on *finding* things which are arranged in alphabetical order, since this is the most common activity involving alphabetical order. There is also some work, in Section 2, on *putting* things into alphabetical order; this is an activity we sometimes need to perform, and it is also very good training for finding things. The unit shows various contexts where things are arranged in alphabetical order – directories, reference books, records of names, newspaper classified advertisements.

Additional material

Essential: Reference books and directories, (for Section 2B), for Section 4C and Extension Work. (Students can go to a library to use these.)

Optional: Local paper, for further practice, Section 3
Small cards, for arranging names in alphabetical order, Section 3

The exercises in the unit provide a model for you to devise further activities, using material and relevant to your students. Once students have mastered the basic skills, the best extension work consists of real tasks where students are doing a job that needs doing, eg

finding things in reference books
writing the class register in alphabetical order
putting enrolment cards in order
adding new cards to a card index in an office or library

Section 1: Check your skill

A assesses how skilful each student is at finding names in a list. Those who need more practice go on to Sections 2 and 3, and then come back to Section 1B, to see if they have improved.

Section 2: Putting things in alphabetical order

A gives increasingly demanding tasks, requiring attention not only to the first letter. For B, it is useful if students can look at actual reference books.

The teaching point in C is that alphabetical lists of names are normally based on the *surname*. If students can see records filed by surname, eg in an office or surgery, it helps to make this clear (and to show how important it is for people with different naming systems to work out how to adapt to a system based on surnames). C1 gives the names with surname first. C2 and 3 require the students to pick out surnames; the first one is done for them to ensure that they know which is the surname.

Section 3: Finding things in alphabetical order

This gives increasingly complex tasks. To find the things, students have to scan one column, then the whole extract.

The advertisements can be exploited for phoning practice, and in other ways. If students all bring a copy of the same paper, this provides lots of opportunities for practising alphabetical order and scanning, as well as many other activities. *Further Practice* can be adapted for your own students and your area. After practice, let students use Section 1B on page 96 to check their progress.

Section 4: Finding the right page in reference books

A

The first part shows various books which use guidewords. It is helpful if students handle actual copies of such books. Regular, short practice sessions on the lines of A2 help students get quicker at finding their way round books. Once students have mastered the basic skill, look for opportunities for students to look up things they, or you, really need to find.

Key

Street Atlas	Answers	Telephone directory	Answers
	1 on the page		1 on the page
	2 before		2 before
	3 after		3 after
	4 on the page		4 on the page
	5 before		5 on the page
	6 after		6 after
	7 on the page		7 after
Atlas	Answers	Dictionary	Answers
	1 on the page		1 on the page
	2 on the page		2 on the page
	3 before		3 before
	4 on the page		4 after
	5 before		5 on the page
	6 after		6 after
	7 on the page		7 on the page
	8 after		8 after

B Key

Problem	Service required	Guidewords in Yellow Pages
a) Your water pipes have burst	4) Plumber	w) Piano tuners—Printers
b) Your eyes need testing	1) Optician	u) Oil Companies—Painters
c) You have to get to the airport very late at night	6) Minicabs	r) Millers—Model Shops
d) You have to move house	2) Removal firm	z) Refrigerator repairs—Rent Officer
e) Your television isn't working properly	3) Radio and TV repair	x) Publishers—Railway equipment
f) You have a broken window	5) Glazier	p) Gift shops—Grocers

Extension work

1 Key

The books mentioned are: Atlas, A-Z Street Atlas, Dictionary, Office Supplies Catalogue, Telephone Directory, Yellow Pages Classified Telephone Directory. Extension Work 3 mentions Encyclopaedia.

2 These problem situations could be tackled by pairs during class time, or given as homework.

Key

Where to find the information:

A Newspaper Entertainments Guide
B Atlas – index
C Street Atlas or Street Map
D Telephone Directory
E Yellow Pages Classified Telephone Directory
F Dictionary
G Local Newspaper
H Yellow Pages
I Telephone Directory

Key

3 Alexander Bell made the first telephone.
The first aeroplane was flown by Orville and Wilbur Wright, in 1903.

Unit 11 Language at work

This final unit shows language at work in two senses; language is used by people at work, and language is put to work by the people who speak and write it, wherever they are.

The sections are independent, and can each be completed in one or two lessons, except for Section 5, which should be worked on little and often. The last section combines activities and skills practised earlier, but otherwise sections can be done in any order.

Section 1: Talking about a job

A – C show how to talk about a job, past or present. Students can relate it in D to their own experience, or that of friends or relatives. Useful homework would be to find out where friends or relatives work and what they do, to tell the class or write down. This can be extended by devising a questionnaire in class, to find out more information than is dealt with in this section, eg full-time or part-time, whether they have lunch at work . . .

Structural points: present simple, 3rd person -s when describing someone else's work, past simple for previous jobs.

The organisation diagram in C helps students to explain how a job fits into a large organisation. You could extend this work by introducing a diagram of the college or institute the students are attending, or the local council. Try giving a blank diagram with a spoken or written text, and letting students label the diagram. An organisation diagram showing the *people* in a hierarchy appears in Section 3.

Section 2: Phoning work when you are ill

Phoning a large organisation involves getting through to the right section or person: this is practised in Unit 2 *Using the Telephone*. Revise this, if necessary. During this section, give students some unexpected situations to deal with – wrong number, extension engaged, etc.

B1
Students listen first for general meaning, and to answer the three questions.

B2
After they have heard it a second time, to notice exactly what is said, some or all of the conversation could be put up on the OHP or blackboard, from students' dictation.

C
Get individuals to phone you first, then arrange paired practice.
This extends the practice to phoning on behalf of someone else. Make sure students understand how to select details from the boxes, in any combination, so that those writing the information down do not know exactly what to expect. See that students practise both roles.

Section 3: Understanding an organisation

People often have no clear picture of the hierarchy in an organisation. They may not know who is responsible for particular areas of work, or who they should go to in particular circumstances. If they do not realise this, they may ask people to do things which they cannot do; a refusal may be interpreted as a personal affront. This section makes students aware of these issues. It encourages them to make good use of information about an organisation.

B Key

a) shifts.
b) telephone their shift supervisor at the beginning of the shift
c) the garage manager
d) Giggiston Bus Company and the trade union

C provides practice of present simple, 3rd person singular and plural. Students can talk about where and when these people work, and their responsibilities – what they can and cannot do.

D can be developed into role play. The teacher as a member of the public or as a fellow employee can try to persuade an individual to do something outside his area of responsibility.

In **E**, a) and b) can be done in pairs, perhaps introduced with work between teacher and a student or between two students, with the whole class listening. For c) students can be grouped in threes, or they can move round the room, changing partners to enable them to talk to a fellow driver and to a garage manager. You can give some students cards, telling them which shift they are on and whether they are free to change to help another driver.

Section 4: Describing a procedure

The words of the librarian can be presented orally, before students read them. Further practice, if needed, could be a gap-filling exercise. For further practice with present simple, 3rd person singular, students can write about the librarian *She deals with new books . . .*

The passive form is introduced in A2. Avoid direct manipulation of the active version to form passive; instead use the procedure diagram in B to cue the passive version. The diagram could be put on OHP. Make sure students understand the conventions of a flow chart. The diagram provides the necessary past participles; many students will need reminding to supply the auxiliary *are*.

The procedure can be described orally a couple of times, then students can write it, as C asks them to.

Further practice: ask questions such as: *What happens after the books are unpacked? What happens to damaged books? How are the catalogue cards filed? Before the books are put on the shelves, what happens?* D consolidates the work. Use it in a different lesson. One new point in this diagram is the use of a singular, *stock book*, which requires both a singular verb, and an article in front: *Then the stock book is filled in.* Another point is the possible omission of the auxiliary when more than one passive verb follows the same subject, eg *The goods are priced and put away.* Look out for opportunities to show the passive in use in procedures.

Section 5: Understanding spoken instructions, asking for an explanation, taking messages

Students need to understand exactly what they are being asked to do. If students have difficulty understanding the practice material on tape, encourage them to listen repeatedly, at normal speed. (Only as a last resort should you repeat things yourself more slowly; if this is necessary, always play the original again afterwards.)

A Understanding spoken instructions
In A1, emphasise the importance of checking that you have understood; point out that this does not require complete repetition of what is said, but selection of the key points.

A2 provides a model.

A3 lets students hear the instructions first to work out the context. (The context would be obvious in real life.) Good students could leave this stage out.

In A4 the group can listen together, and an individual repeat the main points; if you have facilities for individuals or small groups to listen, eg with headphones, several students can do the repeating.

Look for opportunities to ask students to do things, and make sure they check that they have understood, eg fetch something from the office, collect books from the library. Continue such practice in small doses, over a period of weeks.

B Asking for an explanation
Many people are reluctant to ask for an explanation of instructions; they may then fail to do what is wanted.

In B3, stop the tape for a student to ask for explanation. There is not a following explanation on the tape, since we have found that students ask for explanation in various ways, and a recorded explanation which doesn't fit their request is more frustrating than rewarding. It is rewarding for the student if *you* give an explanation which fits their request; here are some suggested replies to *expected* requests.

1 It's in the corridor, just outside the office.
2 The photocopier supervisor will show you.
3 *Justify* means type it with every line ending at the same place.
4 Mrs. Forsyth's the Personnel Assistant, in the Personnel Office.
5 We open at 11.00.
6 I'll show you this afternoon what you need.
7 It's next to the Ambulance Station.
8 He's a young British chess player.
9 Cut them up in small thin strips.
10 Glyphosate is a weedkiller. It's kept in the storeroom.

Again, provide practice in asking for explanation during the course of the classes.

C Taking messages

The amount of support provided for students is gradually reduced. For the first telephone call, C2, they have the notes the receptionist made during the call, and the message she wrote after it. In the next call, C3, they have the notes only, and have to write the message themselves. In C4 they have to make their own notes.

You may want to draw attention to abbreviations as a way of saving time when making notes of a telephone call. Point out different ways of forming abbreviations:

First letters: Pl – please
                   Tues. – Tuesday
First and last letters: cd. – could
Conventional forms: asap – as soon as possible
                      no. – number

D Making Notes

The examples in D show students how they can interrupt, in the right way and at the right time, in order to make a note of what to do. It is better to do this than let the speaker get to the end of a long series of instructions, and then ask him to repeat the lot. However, with some classes you may want to play down this aspect, if they are inclined to interrupt inappropriately already.

The students' aim is to be able to understand and record the main points, first time. However, because of the lack of shared knowledge and expectations, it may be useful to play the instructions through first time to set the scene, and a second time for students to make notes. Get the students to tell you what they have to do, referring to their notes. In a few cases, wait some time before asking, to see if they can reconstruct the instructions from the notes without the help of short-term memory.

As always, incorporate practice into other parts of classes, eg get students to make notes of what to do in a lesson, instead of (or before) writing it on the board. Deliberately start off instructions too quickly for students to write them down, so they have to practise asking you to slow down or repeat.

Section 6: Instructions, warnings and safety notices

The section draws attention to certain features of notices. The important thing here is *comprehension*.

Students are asked to change notices into direct instructions as a means of focusing on the meaning of the original rather than as an activity for its own sake.

Extend the work in the book by doing some practical work in class, eg following instructions for operating a radio, tape-recorder, OHP, etc. Get students to write instructions for some procedure they know. Collect examples of instructions and warnings that students see around them; group together things you must do and things you must not do. Relate informal instructions to formal written ones (eg put the cassette in *cf* insert the cassette). Students can make up instructions for safety in the home, eg if there is a gas leak, the gas must be switched off immediately.

Section 7: Language skills in combination

In B 1–5 the class is working together.

In B 6 you can use magazine pictures of cars and people, with the advantage of colour. Hand a picture of a car, with registration no. visible, to each pair or small group, telling them that this car has been filled with petrol and driven away, and they have to write down details. As soon as you have given out the last picture, start collecting them in, in the same order; this simulates the haste with which the cashier must get the description of the car. Give out pictures of people, and let the pair or group work out a description. Then re-arrange the class so that each student works with a partner who saw a different car and person, to practise telephoning the police to report the incident.

C is a fairly complex exercise, built up in stages. Make sure students understand what to do at each stage. Use the illustration to help to explain.

Tape transcripts

Unit 1 Health

Section 3: *In the doctor's surgery*

3A Listen to a doctor talking to a patient. He's trying to find out what's wrong.
D What can I do for you?
P I've got a very bad pain in my stomach.
D Where exactly is this pain?
P On the left side, fairly low down.
D When do you get it?
P A lot of the time.
D How long have you had this pain?
P About three days now.
D When you get the pain, how long does it last?
P It hurts for a long time, several hours.
D Do you have any other symptoms?
P Yes. When the pain comes, I feel dizzy and sick. I keep shivering.
D Well, I'll have to examine you . . .

3E Listen to the doctor talking to another patient.
D What seems to be the problem?
P It's my eyes. They're sore and itchy. I can't see properly, especially first thing in the morning.
D Let's have a look. Ah yes. You've got conjunctivitis.
P What does that mean? Is it serious?
D It's a highly infectious eye condition. It's very common. It's not serious at all. I'll give you some eye drops.
P How often do I take the drops?
D Morning and evening, until it clears up. Just a few drops in the inner corners of both eyes.
P How long will it last?
D Oh, a week at the very longest.

Section 5: *Hospital*

5B Calling an ambulance
B1 Listen to two 999 calls to the ambulance service:

Call number 1

OPERATOR[1]	Emergency. Which service do you require?
CALLER	Ambulance please.
OPERATOR[1]	What number are you ringing from?
CALLER	861 2411.
OPERATOR[1]	Hold on. I'll put you through.
OPERATOR[2]	Ambulance.
CALLER	Someone has cut her hand very badly. The address is 42, Duncan Drive, Cresswell.
OPERATOR[2]	What number are you ringing from?

| CALLER | 861 2411. |
| OPERATOR[2] | 42, Duncan Drive, Cresswell. We'll come at once. |

Call number 2

OPERATOR[1]	Emergency. What service do you require?
CALLER	Ambulance please.
OPERATOR[1]	What number are you ringing from?
CALLER	861 5266.
OPERATOR[1]	Hold on. I'll put you through.

OPERATOR[2]	Ambulance.
CALLER	There has been an accident in Cresswell at the corner of Westbury Avenue and Larch Road. A motorcyclist has been hit by a car.
OPERATOR[2]	What number are you ringing from?
CALLER	861 5266.
OPERATOR[2]	Corner of Westbury Avenue and Larch Road. We'll come at once.

5C In the Accident and Emergency Unit

C2 Listen to a nurse asking a patient questions. Fill in as much as possible on the registration form on page 9.

N	Now I'd like to ask you some questions. Can you give me your name, please?
P	James Langley.
N	Is that L-A-N-G-L-E-Y?
P	That's right.
N	Your first name is James, Mr Langley. What about your second name?
P	Philip.
N	Can you tell me your address and telephone number?
P	14 Amberley Close, Cresswell, CW6 4PO.
N	Could you spell Amberley for me please?
P	A-M-B-E-R-L-E-Y.
N	14 Amberley Close. Are you on the phone?
P	Yes. 861 2206.
N	What's your date of birth?
P	The fourth of November, 1952.
N	Where were you born?
P	London.
N	What is your religion?
P	I'm a Catholic.
N	And your occupation, Mr Langley?
P	I'm an engineer.
N	Can you give me your next of kin?
P	My wife, Teresa Langley.
N	That's the same address?
P	That's right.
N	Now your doctor's name and address, please.
P	Dr S Pike, 18 Wicks Road, Cresswell.
N	W-I-C-K-S?
P	Yes.
N	Thank you.

Unit 2 Using the telephone

Section 1

1A Listen to these telephone calls, and make notes:
who is the call to?
who is the call from?
what is the purpose of the call?

Call No. 1
A   Derwent Television. Good morning.
B   Good morning. I'd like to arrange for somebody to come and repair my television. The picture keeps jumping.
A   Can I have your name and address, please?
B   Yes, it's Lesley Turner, 36 Harding Drive, Wembley.
A   Lesley Turner, 36, Harding Drive, Wembley. Right. Would 10.30 tomorrow morning be all right?
B   10.30 tomorrow morning. Yes that'll be fine. Thank you very much.

Call No. 2
A   Heston Hospital Pharmacy.
B   Hello. I wonder if you could help me. I have been given some tablets, and on the bottle it says 'take as directed', and I can't remember how many I am supposed to take, and when.
A   What are the tablets called? What name is on the bottle?
B   They're called Filtron.
A   And your name?
B   Mrs P Sanders.
A   Just a moment, Mrs Sanders, I'll check for you . . .

Call No. 3
A   Mr Collins' surgery.
B   Good afternoon. Could I make an appointment with the dentist for a check-up?
A   Yes, when would you like to come?
B   Is there a time free next Thursday, early?
A   Yes, I could give you an appointment at nine – that's the first one.
B   That would be okay.
A   May I have your name?
B   Simon Wright.
A   Simon Wright. Thank you Mr Wright. Goodbye.

Call No. 4
A   Thatcher & Howe. Good morning.
B   Good morning. I'm phoning about a job you advertised as assistant audio secretary.
A   Oh yes. I'll put you through to the office manager.
C   Sheila Hope, here. I understand you are interested in an audio secretary's job.
B   Good morning. Yes. I've been working in a solicitor's office in Manchester, and now I've moved to London with my family I would like to work in a legal firm again.

C   How long were you in your previous job?
B   Two years.
C   Was that your first job?
B   Yes, it was.
C   And were you doing audio typing there?
B   Yes. And I also did some general reception work, and helped on the switchboard.
C   What speed do you type?
B   I got a certificate at 50 words a minute when I was at college. I should think I actually type faster than that now.
C   That sounds good. We are looking for someone to work with the secretary to one of the partners. I'd like you to come in and see me, if you would. Are you free this afternoon?
B   Yes. I could come at any time this afternoon.
C   What about four o'clock?
B   Four o'clock this afternoon. That will be fine.
C   Can I have your name, please?
B   Pamela Barton.
C   I'll see you at four o'clock, then, Miss Barton.
B   Thank you. Goodbye.

Call No. 5
A   Savers Bank, good afternoon.
B   Good afternoon. My name is Fraser. I have arranged to come and see the manager. He sent a letter asking me to come on Wednesday at three, and I'm just ringing to confirm that I can come.
A   It was Mr Fraser, wasn't it? Coming on Wednesday at three. Right, Mr Fraser, I'll tell the manager.
B   Thank you.

Call No. 6
A   This is the South of England Tourist Board. To receive information about weekend break holidays in the South of England, record your name and address when you hear the tone.
B   My name is Emma Nicholls. That's N-I-C-H-O double L-S. My address is 36 Queens Street, Newcastle.

B1
Listen to these four telephone calls. Decide whether they were good, or whether there were difficulties. Tick the comments on page 13 which are right for each call.

Call No. 1
SHOP ASSISTANT	Hammonds. Good morning, can I help you?
CUSTOMER	Oh, yes, I'm ringing up to find out whether you have got some trousers in stock please.
ASSISTANT	Yes, can you give me details, please?
CUSTOMER	Well, they're a new line. They've been advertised all over the place. They're the one that have the advertisement of a man on a sort of brown horse. You know the ones I mean.
ASSISTANT	Er, I'm not quite sure. Could you give me the brand name?

CUSTOMER	I don't know, but they've been advertised everywhere; they're all over the place. I thought you'd know what they are.
ASSISTANT	Are they Rustlers? Or Workwear?
CUSTOMER	Oh dear, I don't know. You're supposed to be the trouser expert.
ASSISTANT	What material are they in?
CUSTOMER	Ah, Corduroy.
ASSISTANT	Yes – what colour and size did you want them in? I'll see if one of the people serving on the floor will know what you're talking about.
CUSTOMER	It's a 32 waist, and I want brown.
ASSISTANT	And what leg length? Average, long or extra long?
CUSTOMER	Oh, I don't know. It's not for me, and I've no idea.
ASSISTANT	I'm afraid we do need a leg length. All trousers . . .
CUSTOMER	Oh for goodness sake. I'm trying to buy some trousers. Are you going to sell me some trousers or are you not?

Call No. 2

A Wallington Green School. Hello.
B Oh, good morning. I'm ringing up about my son, Billy Wright. He's ill, and he won't be coming to school for the rest of this week.
A Oh, I am sorry, Mrs Wright, what's wrong with . . .
B Good morning.

Call No. 3

A Ricky Burns hairdressers. Mrs Burns speaking.
B Oh hello. I'm ringing up about your advertisement in Hairdressers' Weekly, for a trainee hairdresser.
A Oh, yes.
B I'd like to apply for the job.
A Have you got any experience in hairdressing?
B Well, I've had a Saturday job, helping in a salon, and I'd like to become a hairdresser full-time.
A How old are you?
B Seventeen and a half.
A Yes. Could you come in for an interview? Could you come in on Thursday, at eleven?
B Yes, that would be fine.
A Good. Can I take your name?
B It's Emily Johnson.
A Emily, Johnson, right. And your address?
B 46, Fosdyke Road, F-O-S-
A F-O-S-
B D-Y-K-E. Fosdyke Road.
A 46 Fosdyke Road. Right, I'll see you on Thursday then.
B Yes, thank you very much. Goodbye.
A Goodbye.

Call No. 4

A Phoenix Travel Agency.
B Hello, I wonder if you could tell me about flights to Rouen, in France.

A Flights to where in France?

B Rouen.

A Rouen.

B Mm, that's right.

A When do you want to travel?

B I want to go early next week.

A Yes, Monday? Tuesday?

B I want to go, sort of, about the middle of the day on Tuesday and coming back the following Friday afternoon.

A The following afternoon? Wednesday?

B No, no, no Friday, Friday . . .

Section 2 *Making telephone calls*

A Making an appointment

A1 Listen to someone making an appointment. Follow the words on page 14, and see how the prompts help you.

RECEPTIONIST	Dr Green's surgery.
CALLER	Hello. I'd like to make an appointment to see Dr Green.
RECEPTIONIST	Can I have your name please?
CALLER	Yes, it's Joe Carson. The surname is Carson, C-A-R-S-O-N.
RECEPTIONIST	4.30 tomorrow?
CALLER	That's fine. 4.30 tomorrow. Thank you very much.
RECEPTIONIST	Thank you. Goodbye.
CALLER	Goodbye.

Now practise the call with a partner.

A2 Mrs Smith is ringing to make an appointment to see the Headmaster. Her son, Billy Smith, is in Class 3A. Listen and look at the prompts on page 14.

SECRETARY	St Kitts School.
MRS SMITH	Hello, I'd like to make an appointment to see the Headmaster.
SECRETARY	Who is it speaking?
MRS SMITH	This is Mrs Smith. My son Billy is in class 3A.
SECRETARY	Would 4.00 on Wednesday be all right?
MRS SMITH	That's fine. 4.00 on Wednesday. Thank you.
SECRETARY	Thank you. Goodbye.
MRS SMITH	Bye.

Now you practise the call.

A3 Listen to Jane Woods making an appointment to see a solicitor at Rexham Law Centre. Take down the time, and the solicitor's name.

RECEPTIONIST	Rexham Law Centre. Can I help you?
JANE WOODS	Oh yes, thank you. I'd like to make an appointment to see a solicitor.
RECEPTIONIST	Have you seen a solicitor here before?
JANE WOODS	No, I haven't.
RECEPTIONIST	Would five o'clock this evening be all right?
JANE WOODS	Five o'clock this evening. That's fine.
RECEPTIONIST	You'll see Mrs Sullivan.

JANE WOODS   Mrs Sullivan, I see. Thank you very much.

Now you practise the call.

B Changing or cancelling appointments

Call No. 1 Listen to Joe Carson ringing to change his appointment.

RECEPTIONIST   Dr Green's surgery.
JOE CARSON   Hello, this is Joe Carson speaking. I have an appointment with Dr Green and I'm afraid I can't come.
RECEPTIONIST   When was it for?
JOE CARSON   4.30 tomorrow. I'm sorry, I can't come then because I have to collect my neighbour's child from school. Could I please have a later appointment?
RECEPTIONIST   Can you come at half-past five?
JOE CARSON   That's fine. Half-past five tomorrow. Thank you very much.
RECEPTIONIST   Thank you. Goodbye.
JOE CARSON   Goodbye.

Now you practise the call.

Call No. 2 Listen to Mrs Smith ringing to change her appointment.

SECRETARY   St Kitts School.
MRS SMITH   Hello, this is Mrs Smith. I have an appointment with the headmaster, and I'm afraid I can't come.
SECRETARY   When was it for?
MRS SMITH   Four o'clock on Wednesday. My son Billy has got flu, and he's at home. I have to look after him. Could I have an appointment a week later, please?
SECRETARY   What about the same time the following Wednesday?
MRS SMITH   That's fine. Four o'clock on the following Wednesday.
SECRETARY   I hope Billy is better soon.
MRS SMITH   Thank you. Goodbye.
SECRETARY   Goodbye.

Now practise the call.

Call No. 3 Listen to Jane Woods cancelling her appointment at the Law Centre.

RECEPTIONIST   Rexham Law Centre. Can I help you?
JANE WOODS   Good morning. This is Jane Woods speaking. I have an appointment with Mrs Sullivan, at five o'clock this evening. Now everything has got better, and I don't need to see a solicitor. I'm ringing to cancel the appointment.
RECEPTIONIST   I see. Thank you for letting us know. Goodbye.
JANE WOODS   Goodbye.

Now practise the call.

D Finding out

D1 Listen to somebody telephoning to find out information. Fill in the information on the form on page 19.

A   Royal Theatre.
B   Can you tell me, please – what are the cheapest seats available for the play on Saturday evening?

A   Well, most of the really cheap seats are sold out. The cheapest ones we've
    got left are £4.50. There are quite a lot of those left.
B   £4.50. Thank you very much.

Section 3: Dealing with organisations

B Getting through to the right person when you know who to ask for

B2 Listen to this telephone call. You might like to write down what people
   say. You will hear three people: the caller, Mr Thomas, the switchboard
   operator at Coles & Fowler, and the Personnel Officer, Mrs Grant.

SWITCHBOARD	Coles & Fowler.
CALLER	I'd like to speak to the Personnel Officer, Mrs Grant, please.
SWITCHBOARD	It's ringing for you.
MRS GRANT	Personnel Office.
CALLER	Could I speak to Mrs Grant please?
MRS GRANT	Speaking.
CALLER	Oh, Mrs Grant, this is Philip Thomas. I'm ringing . . .

B3 Listen to another call. This time you will hear four people. Work out
   who they are.

SWITCHBOARD	Burtonwood Civic Centre.
CALLER	Could I have the Housing Department, please?
SWITCHBOARD	Trying to connect you.
PERSON 1	Housing.
CALLER	Good morning. Could I speak to Mr Shah, please?
PERSON 1	Just a moment. I'll see if he's available.
PERSON 2	Hello. Dilip Shah speaking.
CALLER	Hello Mr Shah. This is Francis Jones. You rang me yesterday and asked me . . .

B5 Listen to another call. What is different about this call?

SWITCHBOARD	Marks & Spencer; Good morning.
CALLER	Good morning. I'd like to speak to Miss Harris in Accounts.
SWITCHBOARD	Putting you through.
PERSON 1	Dining Room.
CALLER	Oh, I asked for the Accounts Department. I think there's been a mistake.
PERSON 1	I'll try and transfer the call.
SWITCHBOARD	Hello, switchboard.
PERSON 1	Could you transfer this call to Accounts, please?
SWITCHBOARD	Accounts? Right.
PERSON 2	Accounts.
CALLER	Could I speak to Miss Harris, please?
PERSON 2	Speaking . . .

C Getting through to the right person when you do not know who to ask for

C2 Listen to somebody phoning Lesley's department store. Follow the
   words on page 21.

SWITCHBOARD	Lesley's. Can I help you?
CALLER	Hello. I'd like to find out some information about garden chairs.
SWITCHBOARD	Just a moment, I'll put you through to the Garden Furniture section.
ASSISTANT	Garden Furniture.
CALLER	Hello, I'd like to find out some information about garden chairs.
ASSISTANT	Yes, what would you like to know?
CALLER	Have you any folding chairs in stock?

Section 5: Making a sequence of calls

A

Listen to Tony Simpson ringing about his television. As you listen, fill in the details on the Derwent Rental Co. form on page 24.

RECEPTIONIST	Derwent Rental Company.
CALLER	Hello. I rent a television from you. It's gone wrong, and I'd like somebody to come and put it right.
RECEPTIONIST	Can I have your name and address, please?
CALLER	It's Mr Simpson, 12 Heath Avenue, Kenton.
RECEPTIONIST	And your telephone number?
CALLER	865 9073.
RECEPTIONIST	That's Mr Simpson, 12 Heath Avenue, Kenton, and your phone number is 865 9073.
CALLER	That's right. When can you send someone?
RECEPTIONIST	The earliest would be Wednesday, at 2.30.
CALLER	Can you make it a bit later? I won't be in at 2.30.
RECEPTIONIST	Would 5.30 be all right?
CALLER	That's fine. 5.30 on Wednesday. Thank you. Goodbye.
RECEPTIONIST	Goodbye.

B

Now listen to two more calls from Tony Simpson to the Derwent Rental Co. What is his problem? What does he say when he insists that things are put right?

RECEPTIONIST	Derwent Rental Company.
CALLER	Good morning. I arranged with you for someone to call and repair my television yesterday, but nobody came.
RECEPTIONIST	Oh, I'm sorry about that.
CALLER	I'd like to fix another time.
RECEPTIONIST	What about the end of next week?
CALLER	No, I'm afraid that's not good enough. I think it should be sooner than that.
RECEPTIONIST	Well, we're very busy at the moment.
CALLER	But I'd like to watch television and someone should have come yesterday. Please arrange something soon.
RECEPTIONIST	Well, tomorrow, then?
CALLER	Yes, tomorrow at 5.30 would be fine.
RECEPTIONIST	All right, then, tomorrow at 5.30
CALLER	Thank you. Goodbye.
RECEPTIONIST	Goodbye.

Call No. 2

RECEPTIONIST	Derwent Rental Company
CALLER	Good morning. I arranged with you for somebody to come and mend my television yesterday at 5.30, and nobody came. That's the second time that has happened this week.
RECEPTIONIST	Oh, I'm sorry about that.
CALLER	I had specially arranged to be back in time, both days, and then you let me down. It's all been very inconvenient.
RECEPTIONIST	Yes. I realize that. I'll look into it at once.
CALLER	Can you send somebody on Monday?
RECEPTIONIST	Yes, I'll arrange that. What time would suit you?
CALLER	I'd like it to be as early as possible. What time do they start?
RECEPTIONIST	Nine o'clock.
CALLER	Okay. Nine o'clock on Monday then. I hope you won't let me down again.
RECEPTIONIST	Nine o'clock on Monday. I'll make sure somebody comes. Goodbye.
CALLER	Goodbye.

Unit 3 A place to live 1

Section 3: Descriptions

A

Listen to somebody talking about her flat. Look at the plan on page 29 and label the rooms.

It's a three-room flat on the top floor of a three storey block. The kitchen is at the front, between the sitting-room – which is quite big – and the bathroom. There's a separate toilet, and opposite the bathroom door we've got an airing cupboard. There are quite a lot of cupboards built in. There are some in the hall, and also a built-in wardrobe in the bedroom. The bedroom's opposite the kitchen, and the larger room next to the bedroom we use as a dining-room. The bedroom and dining-room have big windows overlooking the back garden. In front of the building is a parking area.

Section 4: Giving directions

Listen to somebody giving directions to his house from the station. On the sketch map on page 30, draw arrows to show where to go, and mark the right house.

Turn left out of the station. Go straight on till you come to the traffic lights, then turn right, into Whitehouse Road. Go straight on and you'll see a park on your right. Turn right immediately after the park, and take the second turning on the left, Smith Street. The house is a little way along, on the right, no. 64.

Section 5: Comparisons

Listen to somebody talking about the house she grew up in and the flat she lives in now. What are the main differences?

Well, I mean, they're so different, I don't really know where to start. I grew up in a huge house – we had nine bedrooms, and the postman thought it was a hotel. It was absolutely huge. And I now live in a small flat. Well, the flat's much, much warmer. In the house I lived in, we had very basic central heating, it wasn't really central heating at all. And it was so cold that you had to put on extra clothes to go to bed at night. The flat is much more modern, and it's cleaner, and it's much less draughty. And it's more convenient. I mean, it's closer to the underground. It's much easier to leave when you go away on holiday. One thing I remember about the house I grew up in was that the floorboards creaked – it was very noisy at night. It was as if there were ghosts walking around on the floorboards. So it was really quite frightening to be there alone at night. And I think adults felt that too. I mean, even my mother didn't like being left on her own late at night.

In an old house, of course, the ceilings are higher and the rooms are larger and more difficult to clean, and much more difficult to keep warm. Well, what else do I remember about the house? It was so different in every way. It was enjoyable, it was fun, and I think that now, I'd find it very difficult to go back to living in a place like that.

Go back and listen again. Write down the words she uses to compare the flat with the house such as *warmer, more convenient.*

Unit 5 A place to live 2

Section 3: *Finding a place to rent – newspaper advertisements*

C
You are going to hear a telephone call from somebody who wants to rent a place. While you listen, look at C on page 48, and tick the correct information.

OWNER	Hello. 887 2836.
CALLER	Hello. I'm ringing about the bedsitter in South Harrow. Is it still available?
OWNER	Yes, it is.
CALLER	Well, could you give me some details please?
OWNER	Yes, it's a large, light room on the first floor, at the front of the house.
CALLER	What are the cooking facilities? Is there a kitchen?
OWNER	There is a small kitchen at the back which you share with two others.
CALLER	Is there a bathroom?
OWNER	Yes. There's a separate bathroom and toilet on the same floor.
CALLER	I'd like to come and see it this evening, after work, if possible. Is six o'clock all right?
OWNER	Fine. The address is 42 Breton Road.
CALLER	42 Breton Road.
OWNER	And your name is –?
CALLER	Lesley Johnson.
OWNER	Right. Six o'clock then. Goodbye.
CALLER	Goodbye.

D

Listen to this telephone call, and write down the information.

A   428 1023.
B   Hello. I'm ringing about the house to let.
A   Ah, yes.
B   Is it still available?
A   Well, several people are coming to see it this evening.
B   I'd like to come today if that's all right. Would 4.30 be convenient?
A   Yes. Your name is?
B   Miss Parker. Could you give me the address?
A   15 Dorman Avenue, Cresswell. It's only five minutes' walk from the station.
B   15 . . . is that D-O-R-M-A-N?
A   That's right.
B   15 Dorman Avenue. Thank you. I'll see you at 4.30.
A   Goodbye.

F

You are going to hear two people talking about a place to rent they have been to see. Look at the advertisements in A on page 47, and decide which place they are discussing.

A   I thought it was nice. It was very quiet.
B   Yes, and it'd be nice to have a garden. There was plenty of room. On the other hand, the outside needed repainting – the paint was peeling off.
A   I suppose so.
B   Actually, for me the main disadvantage is that it's such a long way from the station. Also, there aren't any shops near; we'd miss that after living so near the station and shops.
A   Well, we could try and be better organised about our shopping. I liked it. For one thing, Bob and Jeremy could have a bedroom each, at last; and for another thing, I like the idea of having two rooms downstairs. It means that one can be a dining-room and quiet room, and the other can be a lounge, with the record-player in it.
B   I'm not so sure. On the one hand, it's a nice house with a nice garden. On the other hand, it's not in a convenient position.

Unit 5

Section 5:

B

4 You are going to hear two people talking about one of the houses on page 51 and page 52.

A   The living-room is nice and light. That's good.
B   Well, yes, but the bedroom next to the bathroom is very small. And just think of the biggest bedroom, the colour scheme – purple, with a black ceiling!
A   Yes, I know that room needs repainting. But the decorations downstairs are okay – they have just been done. The kitchen and bathroom are nice. The bathroom is plain white – that's all right; and the fittings are good.

B   The bathroom's rather small.
A   Well . . . You don't really need much space in a bathroom.
B   I'd prefer not to have the toilet in the bathroom. The kitchen was small, too. The sink was okay, with that stainless steel draining board; and the wooden cupboards are good. But there's no room for the fridge, and you couldn't put a table in there – or if you did, you wouldn't be able to open the back door. And there was only one electric socket. That's ridiculous, for a kitchen. We'll have to keep on looking.

Go back and listen to the conversation again. Find out what they now know about the house, which they didn't know from the Estate Agent's information sheet.

Unit 7 Looking for work

Section 1: Looking at jobs

B What does the job involve?
B2 On page 69, exercise B1, there is a list of jobs. Listen to four people talking about the work they do. Find out which job each one has.

1 The first thing to do in the morning is to put out new stock, and tidy everything up. That's why I start work at 8.30. Then when people arrive, they look round; we ask them if they want help, find things for them, take their money and wrap up what they've bought.

2 I have a desk just inside the door, so people can see it, and come and tell me what they have come about. Then I tell them where to go. I'm usually very busy because the phone rings a lot and people want to make appointments.

3 When a department wants to order something, they fill in an order form; the order form comes to me and I keep a record, and send it on. When goods are delivered, we get the invoices. We check that the right goods have been delivered, and then pay the bill. Cheques have to be signed by a director, but I can pay small amounts by cash.

4 I enjoy it because you're with people all the time, and you know you're helping them. The meals are all cooked in the main kitchen; then they come up here on a trolley and I serve them out and take them round. Then I collect up the plates and put them on the trolley to go back down to the kitchen. I do the cleaning in here too. It's important that it's all clean, and if people are getting better, they like to have a chat while I'm cleaning.

Section 2: Finding a vacancy

B
B5 Listen to one of the Job Centre staff talking to someone who wants to apply for two vacancies.

A   You've got two cards there. Which job do you want to try for first?
B   I think I'll try the Filing Clerk.
A   Right. Let me tell you a bit about it. The firm is Fassner & Co Ltd. They're at 422-426 Brislow High Street. Would you be able to get there every day?
B   Oh yes, that's no problem.
A   I'm going to have to ask you some questions about your background. If

you're suitable for the job, I'll phone through to Fassner's, and let you
talk to the Office Manager. I hope you'll arrange a time between you for
your interview. If that happens, you take one of these introduction cards
with you, to the interview. Is that okay?

B   Fine. That's quite clear, thank you.

A   Now they're looking for somebody they can train. No special experience
needed, but they'll want good references.

B   I can give them the names of two referees.

A   Good. Now, can I have your name and address?

B   It's Francis Fernandez. That's Francis – I-S – and Fernandez – F-E-R-N-A-
N-D-E-Z.

A   Fine.

B   The address is 22 Brecknock Road, Brislow.

A   22 Brecknock Road. Good. What are you doing at the moment?

B   I'm unemployed.

A   What was your last job? Can you give me dates, please, and any
experience which is relevant to this vacancy?

B   Well, I was a carpet fitter from . . .

F

F2 Listen to somebody asking if there are any vacancies.

A   Could I speak to the manager, please?

B   I'm the manager. What can I do for you?

A   I'm interested in working in this shop. Have you got any vacancies?

B   Have you worked in a shop before?

A   No, I haven't, but I've been a waitress, so I'm used to dealing with people,
and taking money.

B   Well, we have got a job going. I've got some people coming to see me about
it tomorrow. Can you come and see me tomorrow at 10.30?

A   Yes, certainly. Thank you very much.

Listen to somebody else going into a shop and asking if there are any jobs. She
doesn't give up easily. Notice the words she uses.

A   Excuse me. Could I possibly see the manager for a moment?

B   He's not here just now.

A   When could I see him?

B   What do you want to see him about?

A   To ask about job vacancies.

B   We haven't advertised for any staff.

A   I know that, but I'd like to talk to him about any vacancies which might
come up in the future.

B   Oh, all right then. I'll get him for you.

C   How can I help?

A   I wonder if you might have any job vacancies, full or part-time.

C   Not at the moment except for a temporary vacancy in the produce
section.

A   I'd be interested in a temporary vacancy. How long is it for?

C   About six weeks. If you are interested, fill in this form. Give me all the
details of your experience and let me have it back as soon as possible.

Section 3: Applying

A Applying by phone

A5 Listen to three people phoning up about the job advertised in A4, page 76.
For each call, tick the comments which apply, on the table in A5, page 77.

Call No. 1

SWITCHBOARD	Westons. Good morning.
CALLER	Hello. I want to be a cashier at Westons. I've worked at Martins, and I'm a reliable worker and very keen, and . . .
SWITCHBOARD	Oh yes. I'll put you through to Mr Fortis.
MANAGER	Hello. What can I do for you?
CALLER	Hello. I'm a very good worker, and keen, and I want to be a cashier at Westons.
MANAGER	I see. Have you been a cashier before?
CALLER	Yes, I worked at Martins for a year, and then one of my cousins started his own shop, and I left Martins and went to work with my cousin, but now his shop isn't doing so well, and he can't keep me on, so I'm looking for another job, and I'd like to work at Westons because it is a very good shop.
MANAGER	Could you give me a number I could ring for a reference?
CALLER	Yes. My cousin's phone number is 01 446 5876.
MANAGER	Well . . . Anyway, could you come in and see me? What about tomorrow at ten o'clock?
CALLER	Okay. And I'd like to know if you have good sports facilities for staff. My friend says that a friend of his worked for Westons and played football with a company team. Would I be able to play football?
MANAGER	There will be plenty of time to discuss that if we offer you a job. Please come in tomorrow morning.
CALLER	Sure. See you tomorrow.
MANAGER	And your name?
CALLER	Jeremy Taylor.
MANAGER	Thank you. Goodbye.

Call No. 2

SWITCHBOARD	Westons. Good morning.
CALLER	Good morning. I'm ringing about the Cashier job you advertised.
SWITCHBOARD	Oh yes. I'll put you through to Mr Fortis. He's the manager.
MANAGER	Mr Fortis speaking.
CALLER	Good morning, Mr Fortis. My name is Mrs Harris. I'm ringing about the cashier's job you advertised.
MANAGER	Ah yes. Have you been a cashier before?
CASHIER	Well, I have worked in a newsagent's, and handled cash there.
MANAGER	Could you give me a number I could ring for a reference?
CALLER	The owner was Mr Lovell. His number is 46978.
MANAGER	Right. Thank you. I'll get in touch with him later.
CALLER	Could you tell me – what are the hours?
MANAGER	Well, we work a basic 38-hour working week; the store is open 8.30 to 5.30, Monday to Thursday, Friday is late-night

	shopping – we close at 8; on Saturdays we close at 4.30. There is a rota for staff.
CALLER	Thank you. And what is the pay for the basic working week?
MANAGER	£69.50. Now, could you come in and see me? What about tomorrow at 9.30?
CALLER	9.30 tomorrow morning. That will be fine.
MANAGER	What is your full name?
CALLER	Jane Harris.
MANAGER	Do you know where the shop is? It's 442 High Road, on the corner of Brent Street.
CALLER	The corner of Brent Street. 442 High Road.
MANAGER	Okay, Mrs Harris I'll see you tomorrow morning then.
CALLER	Thank you very much. Goodbye.

Call No. 3

SWITCHBOARD	Westons. Good morning.
CALLER	Good morning, is that Westons?
SWITCHBOARD	Yes. Can I help you?
CALLER	Oh, yes, I'd like to be a cashier, please.
SWITCHBOARD	You'd like to be a cashier? Do you mean you have been offered a job here?
CALLER	No, I read about it in the paper.
SWITCHBOARD	I see. You'd better speak to the manager. Just a moment.
MANAGER	Hello. Mr Fortis speaking. I'm the manager. Can I help you?
CALLER	Yes, thank you.
MANAGER	Yes? What can I do for you?
CALLER	It's about the cashier job.
MANAGER	Yes. Are you interested in the job?
CALLER	Yes.
MANAGER	Have you been a cashier before?
CALLER	Yes, I am a cashier now.
MANAGER	I see. Where do you work?
CALLER	At Symonds Do-It-Yourself Store.
MANAGER	I don't think I know it. Whereabouts is it?
CALLER	It's in Bellingham.
MANAGER	And why do you want to change your job?
CALLER	Well, it's a long way to go every day.
MANAGER	Where do you live?
CALLER	In Handley Street.
MANAGER	Oh, I see. Just round the corner from here. Now, could you give me the telephone number at your present store, so I can ring for a reference?
CALLER	Oh . . . Oh dear, I don't know. I've never had to ring up, so I haven't got the number.
MANAGER	Well, what's the address?
CALLER	I don't actually know the address. I'm not sure what that big road in Bellingham is called. It's a big shop, with a big red sign, saying Symonds, on the main road, near the 45 bus stop.
MANAGER	I see. How long have you been working there?
CALLER	Oh quite a long time.
MANAGER	How long?

CALLER	About, well, mm, I started there last autumn.
MANAGER	Would you give me your name and telephone number? We'll get in touch with you if we want to take it any further.
CALLER	I'm Lesley Freeman.
MANAGER	Lesley Freeman. Yes.
CALLER	35A Handley Street.
MANAGER	It's your telephone number I really need.
CALLER	346-3874. No wait a minute, did I say 346? It's 364.
MANAGER	Thank you. Goodbye.
CALLER	Goodbye.

B Phoning for an application form

3 Listen to someone phoning to ask for a form. In the list on page 78, tick the things the caller says:

A Bryan and Mallory, Good morning.

B Good morning. I'm ringing about the accounts clerk job you advertised in *The Standard* today.

A Just a moment. I'll put you through to that department.

C Mr Simon's secretary.

B Good morning. I've seen your advertisement for an accounts clerk in today's *Standard*, and I'd like to have an application form and further details.

C Oh yes. Can I have your name and address?

B Yes. It's Mr T Watson, 126 Layton Road.

C Can you spell that, please?

B Yes. L-A-Y-T-O-N Road, London N 12.

C Mr T Watson, 126 Layton Road, London N 12. Thank you Mr Watson. Goodbye.

B4 Listen now to someone leaving her name and address on an answering machine, in reply to the next to last advertisement on page 71.

A London Tourist Agency. This is a telephone answering machine. You can record a message. Please speak clearly after the tone.

B I'm ringing about the clerical assistant's job advertised on the seventeenth of March, in the *New Standard*. The reference number is 42/003. Could I please have further details and an application form. My name is Mrs H Kalra, K-A-L-R-A, Flat 4, 23 Westbury Road, W-E-S-T-B-U-R-Y, London NW2.

Unit 9 Interviews

Section 2: *Replying to the letter*

You are going to hear two telephone calls from people who have been asked to come for an interview for a job as a laboratory assistant. Look at the form on page 90, and fill in the right response:

Call no. 1

A Patricia Carrick speaking.

B Good morning, Miss Carrick. My name is Harvey Grant. I applied for the lab. assistant's job. I've received a letter asking me to come for an interview on 22 January, at 10.05. I wonder if it is possible for me to have a later

time, because I'm coming from London, and the train doesn't get in till half past ten.
A Let me see. Yes, you could come at 11.40.
B 11.40. That would be fine. Thank you very much.
A Right, we'll see you then.

Call no. 2
A Personnel Office. Can I help you?
B Yes, thank you. My name is Jane Arnold. I applied for the lab. assistant's job, and I've received a letter asking me to come for interview on 22 January, at 11.15. I'm ringing up to confirm that I can come.
A Thank you, Miss Arnold. We look forward to seeing you.

Section 4: *Preparing for an interview*

C
Listen to people with little or no experience answering interview questions.
A Have you ever done invoices before?
B Well, we did a lot of work on bills in Maths. I haven't done invoices at work but I'm sure I could learn easily.
A Have you ever dealt with the mail?
B No, but I'd like to.
A You know you would have to make the tea?
B Yes, I realise that. I think I'd quite enjoy it.
A How do you see yourself in terms of career opportunities?
B I'm sorry, I don't quite understand. Could you explain, please?
C This is the department.
D I'm sorry I didn't hear that clearly. Could you repeat it please?
Y Are you good with machines?
Z I'm fairly mechanically-minded. If something at home goes wrong, I can usually mend it.

Section 5: *Pattern of an interview*

B1 Listen to this interview and notice the five stages in the pattern.

INTERVIEWER	Ah yes. Come in. Have a seat.
MR TOWNSEND	Thank you
INTERVIEWER	Now you're Mr Townsend? About the sportswear job?
MR TOWNSEND	Yes, that's right.
INTERVIEWER	You live in Bressley?
MR TOWNSEND	Yes, I do.
INTERVIEWER	Now Mr Townsend, tell me what you've been doing.
MR TOWNSEND	I've just finished a course. We had English and Maths as our main subjects. We were taught practical English: writing business letters, taking messages, filing, that sort of thing. The Maths was practical, too. Would you like to hear about that?
INTERVIEWER	Yes, tell me a bit more.
MR TOWNSEND	We worked with calculators, adding machines, wrote out bills and invoices as well as brushing up on general maths. We also had an introduction to computer work.

INTERVIEWER	Right. I see. Tell me something about yourself now, your interests, your plans.
MR TOWNSEND	Well, I'm very keen on sport. I played football for my school. I also play cricket and squash. I've got a motorbike and I'm interested in car and bike maintenance. Shall I go on?
INTERVIEWER	Please do.
MR TOWNSEND	I didn't work that hard at school but I think I've changed a bit since then. I'd like to go into retailing and selling sportswear would be a good start.
INTERVIEWER	Now you'd have to go on a three-week training programme before you'd work behind the counter.
MR TOWNSEND	I'd like that.
INTERVIEWER	You'd have a supervisor who would give you day-to-day tasks other than selling, such as putting out new stock, cashing up at the end of the day. We would expect you to look presentable, not too formal but smart.
MR TOWNSEND	I understand.
INTERVIEWER	Customers pull things about when they're looking through and there's a lot of tidying-up to do.
MR TOWNSEND	I realise that.
INTERVIEWER	You haven't worked before. Are you punctual?
MR TOWNSEND	Yes, I am.
INTERVIEWER	What about days off? Is your health good?
MR TOWNSEND	It's never been a problem so far. I was there every day on the course.
INTERVIEWER	Can you get on with people of different ages and backgrounds?
MR TOWNSEND	I go to an Accounts evening class and there is a great mixture of people there. I get on well with them.
INTERVIEWER	What do you think the problems might be in this job?
MR TOWNSEND	Well, I imagine customers can be a bit difficult. I'd have to watch out for shoplifting.
INTERVIEWER	Do you have any questions you'd like to ask?
MR TOWNSEND	Yes, just one or two. Are there any other branches? Is there a chance I could be moved around?
INTERVIEWER	Yes, we have another shop in Twyford. I doubt we'd send you down there.
MR TOWNSEND	You gave me a sheet of paper with pay and grade and conditions of work on it. Is there any chance of promotion?
INTERVIEWER	Everyone who has the potential to go into management will be promoted. You would start as a trainee for three weeks. Then you're into a six-month probationary period.
MR TOWNSEND	I'm sorry. Could you explain that please?
INTERVIEWER	Well we take you on for six months. If you're up to standard we keep you on permanently. If not, we ask you to go and tell you why.
MR TOWNSEND	I see.
INTERVIEWER	After eighteen months on the counter we'd give you further training. You could be an assistant manager within two years.

MR TOWNSEND	I see. Thank you.
INTERVIEWER	Now we'll write to you within the next couple of days. Thank you for coming in.
MR TOWNSEND	Thank you.
INTERVIEWER	Goodbye. Will you find your own way out?
MR TOWNSEND	Goodbye, yes of course.

Section 6: Further practice

D

Listen to this interview. Discuss the things that go wrong.

A	I've come for an interview.
RECEPTIONIST	Oh, yes. And you are . . . . ? Your name is . . . ?
A	Judith.
RECEPTIONIST	And your surname?
A	Parks.
RECEPTIONIST	Go straight in, Mrs Parks.
MR WATSON	Good morning. Come in Mrs Parks. I'm Mr Watson.
MRS PARKS	Oh, I get it.
MR WATSON	Have a seat.
MRS PARKS	Thanks. I had to stand all the way on the bus. My feet are killing me.
MR WATSON	Now, you live in Prexford . . .
MRS PARKS	Yeah, number 34, Liddall Drive, just off King Street.
MR WATSON	And you're interested in the –
MRS PARKS	– Typist job. I thought about the secretary post but I feel happier doing what I know.
MR WATSON	Your last job was with a firm in Bresswick. Can you tell me more, something about it?
MRS PARKS	Not much to tell really. I was made redundant. It wasn't fair 'cos some who had started work later than me got kept on, but there it is.
MR WATSON	Is there someone in the firm who could give you a reference?
MRS PARKS	I'm not sure who'd be best. There's the Office Manager, now, what's his name? . . . Mr . . . Mr . . . Brinkl . . . Brinkley, I think.
MR WATSON	Now, why are you applying for this job?
MRS PARKS	I'm unemployed. I've applied for lots of jobs, but got nowhere. I'm really fed up about it.
MR WATSON	This job is working in the typing pool.
MRS PARKS	Yes.
MR WATSON	There are four typists in the office here.
MRS PARKS	Oh.
MR WATSON	The Supervisor will give you your work. Some of it is copytyping, some is audio. Can you do audio-typing?
MRS PARKS	Yes.
MR WATSON	You realise that we can't take anyone on unless they take a typing test. Are you willing to take a test?
MRS PARKS	Okay.
MR WATSON	Do you have any questions you want to ask?
MRS PARKS	Only about the money. How much will I get?

Unit 11 Language at work

Section 2: Phoning work when you are ill

B

B1 Listen to somebody phoning to say she is ill. What section does she work in? What is wrong with her? How long will she be away from work?

A Swan Engineering.

B Could I have the Computer Room, please?

A The number is ringing for you.

C Computer Room: Margaret Bowen speaking.

B Hello, Mrs Bowen. This is Anna Boxer. I'm phoning to say that I won't be able to come to work today. I've got a stomach upset, and I keep being sick. I don't think I'll be in tomorrow either.

C I'm sorry to hear that. I hope you'll be better soon. Let us know how you are tomorrow, will you? Goodbye.

B Goodbye.

B2 Go back and listen again, and notice exactly what she says.

Section 5: Understanding spoken instructions, asking for an explanation, taking messages

A Understanding spoken instructions

A2 Listen to two examples of somebody checking that they have understood what to do.

Example 1

A Can you phone the Gas Board, and ask them to come at once? Tell them there was a smell of gas in the hall when we arrived. We've turned the gas off at the mains.

B Right. I'll phone the Gas Board. There's a smell of gas in the hall. We've turned the gas off.

A That's it.

Example 2

A Could you get me a packet of dried green peas, please?

B A packet of dried green beans.

A No. Not beans, peas.

B A packet of dried green peas.

A Right.

A3 Listen to people telling you to do things. For each one, decide where it is, or what the person's job is.

1 Can you go up to the Stockroom, and see if there is a box of large cornflakes? Bring it down if there is.

2 There's a red car out there. Its brakes need fixing.

3 I'm getting short of change. Can you take this fiver, and get me 5p and 10p pieces, please?

4 This is a special delivery to Deerans, in the High Street. Take it right away. Ask for Mr Gerald.

5 Can you check machines 6 and 7? They're both jumping.
6 Would you put clean sheets on bed 6 – there's a new patient coming in – and make the other beds? Thanks.
7 Can you cut up some carrots, and check if the potatoes are cooked, please?
8 There's a box of new records under the table. Would you put them out in the racks?
9 Those pay slips in the corner – can you take them down to Mrs Smith in room 7?
10 I'd like you to type this letter and post it straight away.

A4 Go back and listen again. This time, repeat the main points of what you have to do.

B Asking for an explanation
B2 Listen to two examples of people asking for an explanation.

Example 1
A   Could you take this to the Staff Manager's office?
B   I'm sorry. I don't know where the Staff Manager's office is.
A   It's on the second floor, right next to the lift.

Example 2
A   You need to enter all the new deliveries in the stock book.
B   I'm sorry, I haven't done that before. Can you show me what to do?
A   Come up to the storeroom and I'll show you.

B3 Listen to some people telling you to do things. If you are not sure what to do, ask the speaker to explain.

1 Please put the large files in Cupboard A.
2 I'd like forty photocopies of this paper by lunchtime, on Crown paper.
3 I'd like you to justify all those right-hand margins.
4 I'm afraid I can't help you with this. You'll have to go and see Mrs Forsyth.
5 You're too early; come back at the usual time.
6 Next week we're going to renew the till. Can you get the equipment ready, please?
7 Could you take this over to the Pathology Lab?
8 Would you cut out the photograph in today's paper of Julian Hodgson?
9 I need those carrots cut up please, ready for Carrots Juliennes.
10 All the plants in that bed need to be sprayed with Glyphosphate. Can you get on to that this afternoon?

C Taking messages
C2 Listen to this call and look at the notes the receptionist made and the message she wrote on page 115.

RECEPTIONIST   Barclay and Tyson. Good morning.
CALLER   I'd like to speak to Mr Price, please.
RECEPTIONIST   I'm afraid Mr Price is engaged at the moment. Will you hold?
CALLER   No, thank you. Would you ask him to ring me back as soon as possible? This is Mr Parson, of Folley & Co Ltd.
RECEPTIONIST   I'm sorry, I didn't catch the name of your company.
CALLER   Folley & Co. F-O-L-L-E-Y. The number is 01 592 8661, and it's extension 42.

RECEPTIONIST	Can I check that with you, please? It's Mr Parson, Folley & Co Ltd. You want Mr Price to ring you back as soon as possible, on 01 592 8661, extension 42.
CALLER	That's right.
RECEPTIONIST	I'll see he gets the message. Goodbye.
CALLER	Goodbye.

C3 Listen to this call and look at the notes the receptionist made on page 115. Then write the message.

CALLER	May I speak to Mrs Sharma, in your Food Department?
RECEPTIONIST	I'm afraid Mrs Sharma is away at a conference. Would you like to leave a message?
CALLER	Yes. My name is Glaxo, from Gregson Foods. Could she ring me today, or as soon as possible if she doesn't come back to the office today?
RECEPTIONIST	Right. Can I take your telephone number?
CALLER	Yes. It's 448 2261, extension 12.
RECEPTIONIST	Can I just check that? It's Mr Claxo . . .
CALLER	No, Glaxo. G for George.
RECEPTIONIST	Sorry. Mr Glaxo, from Gregson Foods. You'd like Mrs Sharma to ring you today or as soon as possible, and the number is 448 2261, extension 12.
CALLER	That's right. Thank you.

C4 Listen to these four calls. Make notes, and then write the message.

Call 1

CALLER	Hello. Could I speak to Mrs Gibson?
RECEPTIONIST	I'm afraid she's not here at the moment. Can I take a message?
CALLER	Yes please. This is Antonio's Hairdresser's. Would you tell her that we've got to cancel her appointment on Wednesday. Mr Antonio is ill.
RECEPTIONIST	So the message is to cancel the hairdresser's appointment on Wednesday, because Mr Antonio is ill.
CALLER	That's right. Thank you.
RECEPTIONIST	Thank you. Goodbye.

Call 2

RECEPTIONIST	General Studies Department. Good afternoon.
CALLER	Good afternoon. I'd like to speak to Mrs Fletcher, please.
RECEPTIONIST	I'm afraid Mrs Fletcher is not available just now.
CALLER	Could you take a message for her, please?
RECEPTIONIST	Yes, certainly.
CALLER	This is Corbetts Bookshop. She ordered 20 copies of *Topics and Skills in English*, and they are now in the shop.
RECEPTIONIST	Right; that's 20 copies of *Topics and Skills in English*, in the shop now.

Call 3

| CALLER | May I speak to Mr J Richards, please? |
| RECEPTIONIST | I'm afraid Mr Richards is in a meeting at the moment. Who's calling? |

CALLER	This is Sinclair Electronics. There's a query about an order he sent us. Could you get him to ring me back? The number is Cambridge 56602.
RECEPTIONIST	Cambridge 56602. And your name is?
CALLER	Mrs Wallace. But I'll be out between three and four this afternoon.
RECEPTIONIST	All right, Mrs Wallace. I'll tell him.

Call 4

RECEPTIONIST	Haldane College, Engineering Department.
CALLER	Could I speak to John Parker, please?
RECEPTIONIST	Just a moment . . . I'm afraid he's teaching at the moment. Can somebody else help you?
CALLER	No, this is Susan Parker, John's wife. Do you know when he's free?
RECEPTIONIST	In about an hour and a half.
CALLER	Well, can I leave a message, then? Tell him the car isn't ready, so he should come straight home.

D

D2 Listen to two examples where somebody needs to make notes of what to do. Make notes yourself.

Example 1

A Could you look up in the files the address of Mrs Ghafourian – that's G-H-A-F . . .

B Excuse me, I haven't quite got that. Could you say it again, please?

A G-H-A-F-O-U-R-I-A-N. Her initial is P. She was a student here from 1980 to 82.

B Right, you want the address of Mrs P Ghafourian, a student here from 1980 to 82. I'll look it up.

A Thank you.

Example 2

A Can you call at the Post Office on your way back from lunch? We need some stamps; you'd better get 40 first class and 60 second class . . .

B Just a moment, please. I need to write this down. Right, that's 40 first class stamps . . .

A And 60 second class. Then can you buy two air letters, and a £3 postal order? And while you're at the shops, could you buy a jar of coffee? Thanks.

B Okay. I'll get forty first class and sixty second class stamps, two air letters, a £3 postal order and a jar of coffee.

A Fine.

D3 Go back and listen again to the two examples. Notice ways of asking somebody to slow down or repeat.

D4 Listen to people telling you what to do. Make notes of the main points.

1 Telephone Mrs Cummings, please, and arrange for her to come in as soon as possible for a blood test. Her number is 963 4026.

2 Could you enter some dates in the diary please. On Monday, there's a

meeting at nine in the morning of the Staff Committee; then Mr Simons is due at 10.30. On Tuesday at 11.30 Mr P S Patel has an appointment.

3 Phone Mr Smith, will you? He wants to see the Personnel Officer, so make an appointment for him to come here to the office some time on Tuesday or Wednesday. Then you can go to the Stationery Room, and get some large envelopes, large brown ones, that is. We'd better have about 50. Then get on to the filing. There's a pile of things on the table to be put away.

4 Can you look up in the latest catalogue, and find out prices for
   a Sperry-Remington typewriter SR101,
   an Olympia portable 39 typewriter,
   a Sinclair calculator – the cheapest one,
   and a Honitsu table-top photocopier.

5 The workshop have just finished two cars. Can you phone the owners and tell them they can come and collect their cars – it's a red Granada, reg. TUM 224S, and a brown Cortina, JJL 980X. The owners' names and phone numbers are in the file.

Section 7: Language skills in combination

B

Listen to an experienced cashier telling a new cashier what to do if a driver puts petrol in his car and drives away without paying.

You phone the police right away. There have been so many cases round here lately, sometimes the same driver more than once. Try and see what the driver looks like, but anyway get the registration number, and get a description of the car – what colour it is, what make, anything noticeable about it . . .

B5 Listen to a cashier phoning the police. As you listen, fill in the information on the REPORT CHART FOR NON-PAYMENT on page 119.

POLICE   Police.
CASHIER   This is Greenhill Garage here, Station Road.
POLICE   Oh yes.
CASHIER   A driver has driven off without paying for petrol.
POLICE   When did this happen?
CASHIER   About five minutes ago.
POLICE   Have you got any details?
CASHIER   Yes, it was a woman driver in a brown Mini, registration number ENM 422T. She had short fair hair and glasses. She drove off without paying £10.25.
POLICE   Okay. Thanks for letting us know. We'll see what we can do.
CASHIER   Thanks. Goodbye.

C Breakdown 1

You are the cashier on night duty. Listen to a call from a driver. As you listen, write down the information on the BREAKDOWN SERVICE FORM, on page 121.

CASHIER   Greenhill Garage.
DRIVER   Oh, thank goodness. I believe you have a 24-hour breakdown service.

CASHIER Yes, that's right. What's the problem?

DRIVER My windscreen wipers have broken. They won't work at all, and I simply can't see out. It's pouring with rain. I can't drive the car without the wipers.

CASHIER Well, we can send somebody to see if they can be mended. Could you give me some details? Your name is . . . ?

DRIVER Farley, F-A-R-L-E-Y.

CASHIER Mr Farley. And what is your car?

DRIVER It's a Jaguar XJ6.

CASHIER What colour?

DRIVER Black.

CASHIER And the registration number?

DRIVER LUF 644X.

CASHIER Was that MUF?

DRIVER No, L for lunch; LUF 644X.

CASHIER Right, I've got that. Now, where are you? Where is the car?

DRIVER It's on the North Circular Road, just opposite the big Smiths factory . . .

CASHIER Okay, Mr Farley. I'll get a mechanic to you in about half an hour.

DRIVER Thank you very much.